Lewis would describe himself as a creative young British writer, who since becoming a father at 21, has developed a keen passion for storytelling. Originally from the Isle of Wight, Lewis has spent much of his life living and working between Kent and London, in which time he served in the British Army Reserve for several years. Much of Lewis' writing inspiration derives from time spent with his son Teagan and also travelling. It is Lewis' dream to travel the world and in doing so follow in the footsteps of a longstanding idol of his, the renowned explorer Michael Palin.

LEWIS RAY

The Elf That Couldn't Stop Gaming

AUSTIN MACAULEY PUBLISHERS
LONDON * CAMBRIDGE * NEW YORK * SHARJAH

Copyright © Lewis Ray 2024

The right of **Lewis Ray** to be identified as author of this work has been asserted by the author in accordance with sections 77 and 78 of the Copyright, Designs and Patents Act 1988.

All rights reserved. No part of this publication may be reproduced, stored in a retrieval system, or transmitted in any form or by any means, electronic, mechanical, photocopying, recording, or otherwise, without the prior permission of the publishers.

Any person who commits any unauthorised act in relation to this publication may be liable to criminal prosecution and civil claims for damages.

A CIP catalogue record for this title is available from the British Library.

ISBN 9781035848744 (Paperback)
ISBN 9781035848751 (ePub e-book)

www.austinmacauley.com

First Published 2024
Austin Macauley Publishers Ltd®
1 Canada Square
Canary Wharf
London
E14 5AA

To my wonderful son Teagan, without whom I would truly be lost. You have given my life purpose and for that I owe you the world. I hope you enjoy this story I wrote for you, my (slightly) gaming mad child!

To my grandad Ray, who I wish could be here with me today. You are forever in my thoughts and I really hope that I have done you proud!

I would, of course, like to thank Austin Macauley Publishers for giving me the opportunity to help bring my visions to life! It is an absolute pleasure to work with them!

The foremost rule of "elf and safety";
"All toys must be tested!"
And so each time a gift is made,
It's meticulously inspected!

A team of elves is standing by,
Trained to test for flaws.
Once it's deemed a toy complies,
It's then wrapped and sent forth.

Such a job may sound quite boring,
Inspecting toys each day.
For one elf though, work was rewarding,
In fact, his work was play!

TESTING DEPARTMENT

Giz the elf was gaming mad,
New consoles he would test.
Merch-obsessed and hoodie-clad,
His setup was the best!

Neon lights lit up his station,
Where 4K screens await.
A gaming chair he'd meanwhile play in,
Whilst merch surrounds his space.

"Gaming Giz" he too was known,
To those who watched his streams.
But, for those elves near his "zone"
He was the noisiest in the team!

"Woooah!" you'd sometimes hear Giz cry,
"Did you see that guys?" he'd say.
At other times, he'd yell "nice try!"
Much to his colleagues' dismay.

The elves would end each day relieved,
Giz's noise left them irate.
Giz himself meanwhile wouldn't leave,
And would instead game on till late!

Giz's obsession was no doubt strong,
But worse was yet to come!
When VR headsets were to come along,
He would then have way more fun!

Giz's shouts grew louder now,
As he explored virtual worlds.
He seemed to chat forever somehow,
With virtual boys and girls.

Through wondrous lands, his journeys went,
Across seas and into space.
Endless hours the young elf spent,
"Away" from his workplace.

Giz would each time return to work,
To find consoles piled high.
No choice he'd have but to go berserk,
And test them through the night!

As time went on, Giz rested less,
Whilst most days he didn't eat.
His zone meanwhile had become a mess,
As he'd barely leave his seat.

Then, one cold December eve,
He gamed longer than ever.
Along with a friend called "SimplySteve",
The two explored VR together.

Steve took Giz to past events,
From caveman to Egyptian times.
"This is wicked!" a stunned Giz went,
Whilst watching mammoths stomp by.

Suddenly... it all went black,
And off the headset came.
Before Giz cross-armed elves glared back,
Whose festive clothes had changed.

"Is Christmas cancelled?" tired Giz croaked,
Whilst rubbing his achy eyes.
"It's January!" a gruff elf spoke,
Much to Giz's surprise!

The exhausted elf appeared concerned,
"But why tell me so late?"
"Because Giz it is time you learned,
That your ways make us irate!"

Santa meanwhile was mortified,
And summoned Giz for a chat.
"You've let down boys and girls worldwide,
I'm afraid I can't have that!"

And so, young Giz would game no more,
With dolls he instead plays.
Though glum, he's learned one thing for sure:
It's wrong to game all day!

THE END

Happy Birthday Legend !!!
Love Jacob, Voni & Pablo xxx

Portraits of American Bikers: Inside Looking Out

THE FLASH COLLECTION II

BEVERLY V. ROBERTS

Beverly Roberts 2017

Portraits of American Bikers: Inside Looking Out
The Flash Collection II (First U.S. Edition 2010)

Published in the United States by Flash Productions, LLC
P.O. Box 34, Birmingham, MI 48012-0034
www.flashproductionsllc.com
email: flash@flashproductionsllc.com

Copyright © 2010 Flash Productions, LLC & Beverly V. Roberts
All photographs Copyright © 2007-2010 Beverly V. Roberts
Outlaws MC ® Registered Trademarks printed under License

Printed in the United States of America

All rights reserved. With the exception of quoting brief passages for the purposes of review, no part of this book may be used or reproduced in any manner in any media, or transmitted by any means whatsoever, electronic or mechanical (including photocopy, film or video recording, internet posting, or any other information storage and retrieval system) without the prior written permission of the publisher.

Disclaimer: In the biker culture of 1960s the swastika was prominently displayed. Our purpose is to show the biking culture as accurately as possible; omitting or editing images that contain swastikas and/or other controversial content would not be historically accurate.

Library of Congress Control Number: 2009938518

ISBN: 978-0-615-32785-3

Acknowledgements

Project Coordinator & Liaison for the A.O.A. (American Outlaws Association): Daniel " Big Dan 1%er" Fulghum

Cover Design by Michael "Mike 1%er" Hansen - Outlaws MC Germany

Book Title by Don "Jingles 1%er" Foshey

Introduction by Bill Hayes

Technical Advisors for this book: Big Dan 1%er, Flapper 1%er, Lenny 1%er, Surfer 1%er, Fuzz 1%er and Stitch 1%er

Photo Editing by E. Sapwater & Tom Roberts

"Biker's Names" by Richard "Bingo" Crosby

"An American Biker" by Ironhorse Writer - Laurence P Scerri

Flash Collection Photos (1960s) by Jim "Flash 1%er" Miteff

Flash Collection Photos (2008-2009) by Beverly V. Roberts

Photo of Flapper 1%er (2009) by "Mrs. Flapper"

Special thanks to Sue "Mama Bear" Clark - for all your love and support
and to Red River Paper (www. redrivercatalog.com)

BIKER'S NAMES

By Richard "Bingo" Cosby
Wisconsin Confederation Of Clubs

I'll bet I've met ten thousand bikers! Many with "names" the same
And I always wondered -how in the hell he got that goofy name!
I've met a dozen "Spiders" and "Wild Bills" -a dozen more
"Crazy" this, and "Crazy" that,--"Bigs" and "Littles" by the score
I knew a "Rocker", a "Burrito", a "Papa Snake", a "Weasel" and a "Frog.
A "Goat", a "Bear", "Big Animal", a "Tiger", and a "Hawg".
I know a "Buzzard", a "Turkey", a "Hawk", a "Duck", a "Goose"
A "Polock", "Swede", and "Dago" - a "Shovel", "Rat" and Moose.
There's "Solo", "Shooter", "Hungry", "Flapper" and a "Crank"
"Boonie, "Dozer", "Junkyard", "Dirty Doyle" and "Tank".
"Old Man Pete", a "Maverick", a "Butcher" and a "Slash"
"Soneface", "Greaseball", "Taco", "Skeeter" and a "Crash".
There's a "One Eye", "Nubs" and a "Chopper" - a "Weiner" and a "Louse"
"Kind Brother", "Surfer", "Snoopy, "Criminal Chris" and "Moose".
"Private John and "Cowboy" - "Hundred Proof and "Dirty Dan"
"Stairway Harry", "Jingles", a "Hitler", "Skull" and "Pan".
"Joe The Jag", "Kingfish", "Spike", "Ghetto" and a "Brew"
A "Wizard", "Suicide, "Killer", a "Tiny" and a "Heavy" too.
One "Claim Jumper", a "Chad", "Poppy", "Speed" and "Shoe"
"Super, "Snatch", "preacher", a "Yankee and a "Rebel" too.
There's some that really blow my mind! Some that really puzzle me!
"Douche Bag", "Bugs" and "Maggot -- "ganggreen" and one "V D"!
"Barf", "Skidrow", "Pervert", "Dickless", "Weird" and "Crud"
"Vulture", "Puke", "Dog's Breath", a "Dirt", a "Slime" and "Mud".
There's a "Rotten", a "Scumbag", a "gargoyle" and a "Worm"
A "Dickhead", "Towbar", "Lousy", a "Filthy", "Ded" and "Germ"
One they call "Greased Lightning" - a "mad", A "Freak", a "turd".
And for every crazy name that I forgot - I'll bet there's two I haven't heard!
I could go on and on - and I bet you know a few.
I know how I got MY name --- Now stop - and think --- Do YOU?
Bingo...

Don "JINGLES 1%er" Foshey

1952-2008
36 year member - Outlaws MC Milwaukee

Two things come to mind when I think of Jingles. First, the day we met. It was as though I had known him forever. We bonded instantly as we began work on *Portraits of American Bikers: Life in the 1960s*. We had the same vision; to honor my Father and the other early members of the Outlaws MC by publishing these photographs. The second thing that comes to mind is the day that I last saw Jingles. Little did any of us know at the time, Jingles had cancer. Soon after we started work on the first book he began treatment for the disease. A lot of people would have stopped right there and nobody would have blamed them. Not Jingles. While he battled cancer for the next year he also worked side by side with me on that first book. It was a proud moment when we finished the book that would debut at the Milwaukee Art Museum during the Harley 105th Anniversary celebration in Milwaukee, Wisconsin. As it turned out, Jingles was in the hospital recovering from surgery the day our exhibit opened at the MAM. Tom and I went to see Jingles at the hospital where we presented him with the first book off the press. He passed away three weeks later.

This book is dedicated to Jingles 1%er with my deepest love and respect. He is gone but will never be forgotten.

Beverly V. Roberts

In loving memory of Flash 1%er, Jingles 1%er, Stairway Harry 1%er and "Uncle" Moses 1%er

G.B.N.F.

Introduction

By Bill Hayes

Author, Motorcycle Culture Historian, and American Biker

It's been a long time since the mainstream media first discovered the motorcycle club culture—and its seductive appeal. That particular journey has seen our lifestyle "creatively" populated by villains, clowns, cutthroats, buffoons, deviants, sadists, criminals, badasses, and everything in between. But no matter what characters or images the writers, reporters, producers, and directors have devised to represent our lifestyle, the bottom line is that people love it. They fear it. And deep down—in those trembling, vicarious bones—they would give anything to be a part of it.

Anything, for just one ride in an endless pack, hammer-down in the screamer lane of some interstate.

Anything, to walk proudly into a bar or an event with a set of colors on—recognized colors that are not given, but earned, through serious effort, blood, and brotherhood.

Anything, to be able to call a brother at any hour of the day or night when they needed help with *anything*, and to know that their back is covered.

Anything, to be intimate with the powerful "family life" that is truly enjoyed—and unapologetically embraced—by so few.

But envied or not, this way of life often comes at a high price. A patch on one's back can translate into a titillating target for law enforcement, as well as media. For a variety of reasons—commercial gain, high-profile PR, and political pandering among them—both have dipped to sordid lows in their pursuit of the "biker" essence. Those clowns and buffoons of the old "B" biker movies have increasingly given way to the cutthroats and the criminals. Entire television networks use shows about the *presumed* inside of the motorcycle clubs as their commercial anchors. Dozens of books and productions glorify the "dirt-digging" adventures of undercover law enforcement infiltrators, turncoats, and snitches.

We're hunted using a simple template: focus on a single alleged illegal act; find a disgruntled member (or simply a shrouded actor) to talk about it; get some stock public film footage or stills of patches; and—boom! A blanket condemnation of an entire club—or the whole culture. The same template could of course be used for virtually every other large group or coalition—including big-league urban police departments and the United States Congress. But those types of exposés don't have the same attraction as those dealing with bikers and motorcycle clubs. Maybe no one really wants to have a vicarious fantasy that involves a cop or a senator.

Another bottom line is evident here: While most of these "monster exposés" don't produce many tangibles in the way of the legally-righteous elimination of crime, they *do* produce a lot of media. But not media like *this* book. The photos and the people in this book are *real*. As is the essence and feeling and history they project. The photos here were born of one of the most influential eras in the evolution of the American biker—the social sledgehammer that was the '60s. But they also prove the timelessness of this culture. They prove that the pure abandon, rebel-at-all-costs, hell-raising brotherhood that gave birth to the American biker in the World War II days existed and flourished in the '60s. And still exists today. In exclusive circles, that is.

As a member of the Outlaws Motorcycle Club, Jim "Flash 1%er" Miteff momentarily caged the spirit of their 1960s biker world into the lens of his camera; creating images that roar from the middle of those exclusive circles—like kings of the jungle on the prowl.

This is who we are!

This is what we do!

The first volume of the Flash Collection, *Portraits of American Bikers: Life in the 1960s*—compiled lovingly and respectfully by Miteff's daughter, Beverly—released those immortal images into our culture in an unprecedented way. But while Miteff may have been rooted in the '60s, the gut-level punch of his work shows who the Outlaws have been for a very long time; what they have done for a very long time; and what they will be doing for a long time to come.

This second volume in the Flash Collection, *Portraits of American Bikers: Inside Looking Out* bears—and bares—the soul of *all* bikers. Past, present, *and* future.

Cycle-Rama – Detroit Michigan, circa 1966

Detroit, MI - 1968

Tommy Tucker 1%er (first President of the Detroit Chapter of the Outlaws) sitting on J.C. 1%er

Flash 1%er – Circa 1966

Detroit, MI – circa 1966

Detroit, MI – circa 1967

Wild Bill 1%er

Lester (club hang-around)

National Run to Bong Recreational Area near Kenosha, WI

Detroit, MI – circa 1967

Lenny 1‰er (2nd from left) at the National Mud Run

Fat Cowboy 1%er (3rd from right), Papa Snake 1%er (2nd from right)

Deke 1%er (3rd from left), Serb 1%er (4th from left), Big Daddy 1%er (center), Lenny 1%er (2nd from right), Little Adolf 1%er (right)

Tommy Tucker 1%er – Detroit, MI

Outlaws and Centaurs partying at the Centaurs clubhouse before the party was crashed by a rival club

The Centaurs clubhouse, the morning after the party

Flash 1‰er on the ferry between Muskegon, MI and Milwaukee, WI

Karate 1%er and his ole lady on the ferry between Muskegon, MI to Milwaukee, WI

On the ferry between Muskegon, MI and Milwaukee, WI

Brian 1%er (center), Moses 1%er (2nd from right), Karate 1%er (right)

Wild Bill 1‰er (2nd from right), Riaco 1‰er (right)

Jake of the Vagabonds MC - New Baltimore, MI

Moses 1‰er (left), Little Adolf 1‰er (center)

Downtown Detroit, MI – circa 1966

Little Adolf 1‰er (2nd from left), Big Daddy 1‰er (center) Serb 1‰er (2nd from right), Deke 1‰er (right)

Lenny 1%er (2nd from left in 2nd row)

Fat Cowboy 1%er (2nd from left), Joey 1%er (2nd from right)

National Run to Bong Recreational Area near Kenosha, WI

Gregg (Brothers MC), Harry (hang-around), Tommy Tucker 1%er (retired) and Lester (Brothers Prospect) - circa 1970

Karate 1‰er (left)

Hip To It 1%er (4th from left)

Book Cover in full
Donnie Burns 1%er (left), John Morse 1%er (2nd from left), Crash Cup 1%er (3rd from left), Kenny Brown 1%er (2nd from right)

Cycle-Rama – Detroit Michigan, circa 1966

Crazy John 1%er (left), Johnny 1%er (right)

Riaco 1%er (left)

Half Breed 1%er and his ole lady

Little Adolf 1‰er (left), Big Daddy 1‰er (2nd from left), Karate 1‰er (3rd from left), Serb 1‰er (3rd from right), Tony Bee 1‰er (2nd from right), Brutus 1‰er (right)

Moses 1‰er & Mama Moses

Bones 1%er

Deke 1%er (center), Big Daddy 1%er (right of center)

Tony Bee 1‰er (left)

Wild Bill 1%er (in back)

Detroit, MI – circa 1967

Detroit, MI - circa 1967

Wild Bill 1%er (center), Riaco 1%er (right)

Cycle-Rama, Detroit, MI – circa 1967

Flash 1%er (Center)

At Kaiser's wedding

Johnny Ginger, host of Detroit's Curtain Time Theatre (a kid's show that ran from 1956-1967 on WXYZ-TV) with Flash 1%er

*Flapper 1%er (center) and Surfer 1%er (right) sign a copy of Portraits of American Bikers: Life in the 1960s for Doc 1%er
Photo by Beverly V. Roberts 2008*

Bob "Moses 1%er – retired" Dick
photo by Beverly V. Roberts 2009

Lenny 1%er
photo by Beverly V. Roberts 2008

Flapper 1%er (left), Papa Snake 1%er (2nd from left)
Reprinted from Portraits of American Bikers: Life in the 1960s

Flapper 1%er
photo by "Mrs. Flapper" 2009

Fat Cowboy 1%er (left), Surfer 1%er (center), Half Breed 1%er (right)
Reprinted from Portraits of American Bikers: Life in the 1960s

Greased Lightning 1%er & Surfer 1%er
photos by Beverly V. Roberts 2008

Flapper 1%er (2nd from left) – Daytona Beach, Fl
photo by Beverly V. Roberts 2009

"We may be here for a short while, gone tomorrow into oblivion or until the days come to take us away. Whatever part you play, be remembered as part of a legacy...of sharing dreams and changing humanity for the better. It's that legacy that never dies"

Author Unknown

Jim "Flash" Miteff – 1967

Beverly V. Roberts – 2009

Back in the 1960s, using a Graflex Speed Graphic Press Camera, Jim "Flash" Miteff shot several hundred photographs of the Outlaws 1%er MC. The photographs in this book were specially selected from his collection. These never before published images are taken directly from the original 4 x 5 negatives that had been in storage for over 40 years.

The Outlaws Motorcycle Club began in McCook County, Illinois USA in 1935 and is currently one of the largest motorcycle clubs in the world with chapters all over the United States, Canada, Europe, Australia and Asia.

Not your typical "girl next door", Beverly Roberts, the daughter of Outlaw biker Jim "Flash 1%er" Miteff, was riding on motorcycles before she could walk.

When Beverly was as young as eight years old, while helping develop the pictures her father took of the Outlaws Motorcycle Club, she dreamed one day these photos would be shared with the world.

A retired stockbroker, Beverly owns Flash Productions, LLC, the publishing company named after her late father.